PENGUIN BOOKS

THE BOOK OF TERNS

Peter Delacorte was born in New York City and attended Princeton University, where he majored in English, won the F. Scott Fitzgerald Prize for creative writing in 1967, and met his coauthor, Michael C. Witte. A freelance writer, Mr. Delacorte has written widely about rock and roll and has worked at WABC-FM. In 1972 he moved to California, where he has written on diverse subjects and has been at work on a screenplay. He and his wife live in San Francisco with a dog, two cats, and several hundred tropical fish.

Michael C. Witte is a native of St. Louis, Missouri, and a 1968 graduate of Princeton University, where he was art editor of the campus humor magazine. Since 1969 his drawings have appeared frequently in *Time* magazine; one of these drawings was selected as the Best Feature Cartoon of 1972 by the Newspaper Guild of New York. Mr. Witte coauthored with baseball player Tug McGraw the nationally syndicated comic strip "Scroogie," which charted the foibles of life in professional sports. Mr. Witte is presently on the executive committee of the Cartoonists Guild. He lives and works in New York City's Greenwich Village with his psychologist wife and a funny dog named Jasper. He owns no birds.

The Book of

BY
PETER DELACORTE
AND
MICHAEL C.WITTE

Terns

PENGUIN BOOKS

Penguin Books Ltd, Harmondsworth,
Middlesex, England
Penguin Books, 625 Madison Avenue,
New York, New York 10022, U.S.A.
Penguin Books Australia Ltd, Ringwood,
Victoria, Australia
Penguin Books Canada Limited, 2801 John Street,
Markham, Ontario, Canada L3R 1B4
Penguin Books (N.Z.) Ltd, 182-190 Wairau Road,
Auckland 10, New Zealand

First published 1978

LIBRARY OF CONGRESS CATALOGING IN
PUBLICATION DATA
Delacorte, Peter.
The book of terns.
1. Puns and punning. 2. American wit and humor,
Pictorial. I. Witte, Michael C., joint author.
II. Title.
PN6231.P8 D4   818'.9'1407   78-18199
ISBN 0 14 00.4905 3

Printed in the United States of America by
The Murray Printing Company, Westford, Massachusetts
Set in Alphatype Helvetica

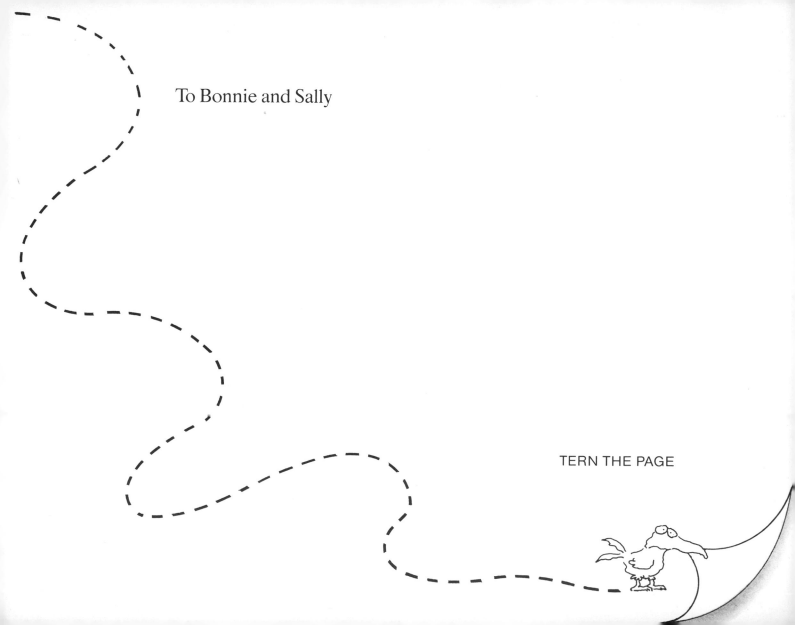

To Bonnie and Sally

TERN THE PAGE

tern   *n.* [of Scand. origin; akin to Dan. *terne*]: any of numerous seagulls—*Sterna* and related genera—that are smaller and slenderer in body and bill than typical gulls, with narrower wings, forked tails, and black cap

COMMON TERN

TIME

TERN OF THE CENTURY

TERN OF FORTUNE

TERN ON

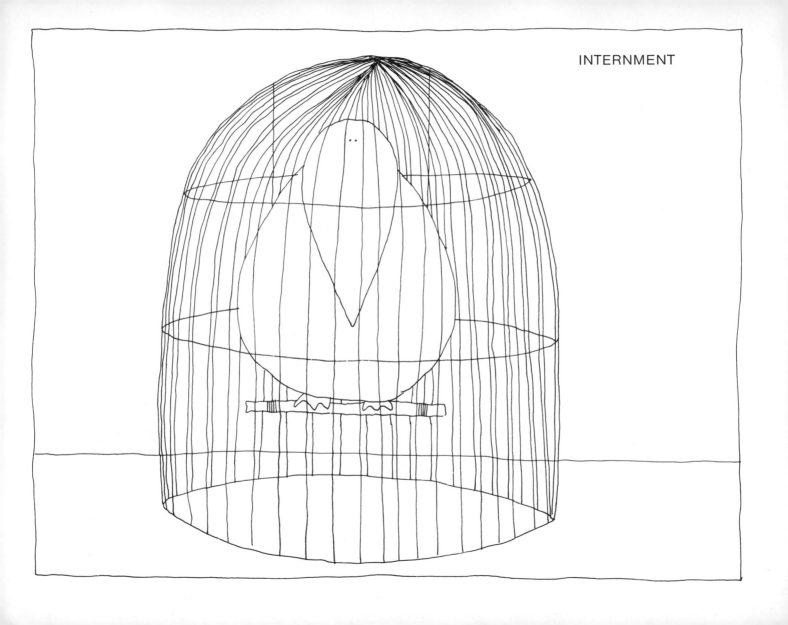

ATTERNEY

TERN LOOSE

TERN OUT OK

TERN CATHOLIC

SLATTERN

TERNPIKE

LANTERN

RETERN
OF THE
NATIVE

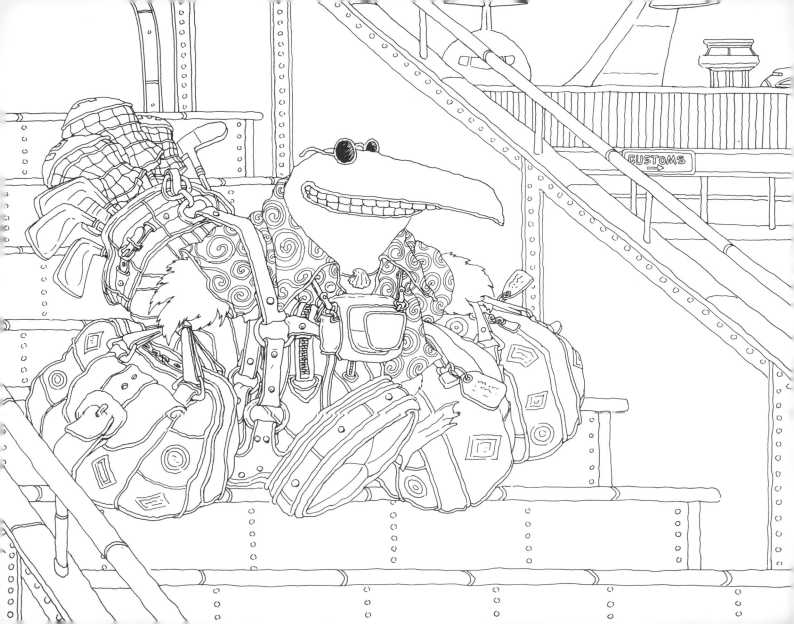

EASTERN

WESTERN

鈴木春信画

INTERNATIONALS

TERN OF BATTLE

TERN TAIL

TERN OF THE SCREW

TERNKEYS

TERN AT BAT

TERNAMENT

FRATERNITY

TERN PRO

A TERN FOR THE BETTER

A TERN FOR THE WORSE

LEFT TERN

COMINTERN

TERN OLD BEFORE HIS TIME

TERN IN

DRAMATIC TERN

TERN OF PHRASE

A STRANGE TERN OF EVENTS

PRETERNATURAL

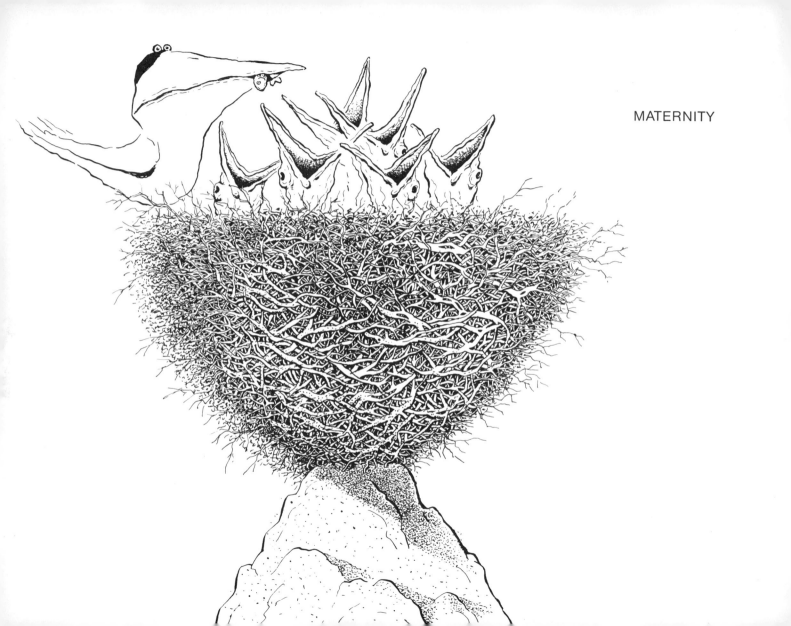

MATERNITY

PATERNITY

TWISTS AND TERNS

TERN
OF THE
WHEEL

POINT OF
NO RETERN

TERNING
POINT

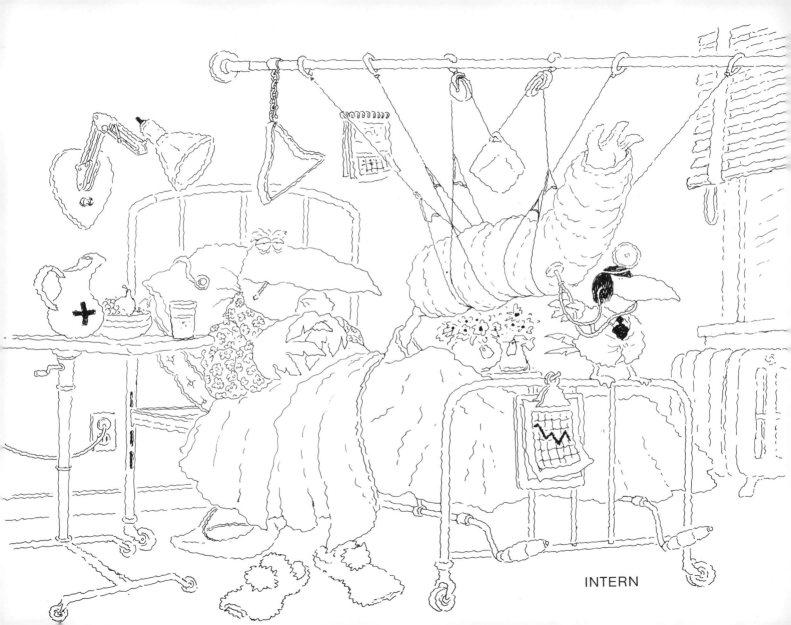

INTERN

ETERNITY

NOCTERNAL

360° TERNS

U-TERN

NO U-TERN

A SOFT ANSWER
TERNETH AWAY WRATH.

TERNING THE OTHER CHEEK

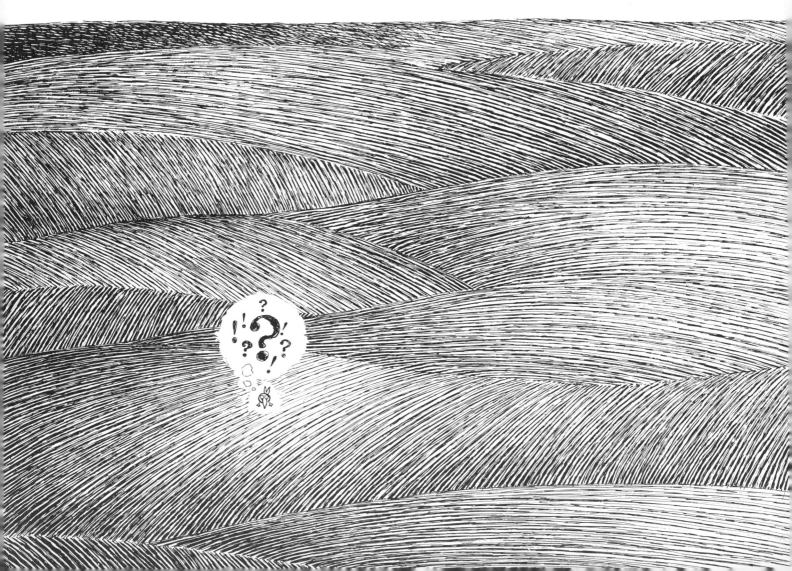

TERN OF THOUGHT

$$My = \int_o^b \frac{x}{2} \cdot X \cdot \frac{dy}{c} = \frac{1}{2} \int_o^b \frac{y^4}{4P^2} \cdot dy = \frac{1}{8P^2} \int_o^b y^4 \cdot dy = \frac{1}{8P^2} \left[\frac{y^5}{5} \right]_a^b + \frac{db^2}{\pi r^2} \cdot$$

$$\frac{dI}{dy} = K \left[\frac{(y^2+r^2)^2 - 3y^2(y^2+r^2)}{\sqrt{\Delta 2y + r^y}} \cdot \frac{x}{y}^{16} + \frac{\varepsilon}{3} \frac{\sqrt{x^2+b}}{LBJ} \right\rangle \frac{3x}{mcw} +$$

$$\left(\frac{\mu(2T+\Delta T)}{dT \cdot d\theta} \right) + C/y^2 \cdot \frac{(\sqrt{\infty})^y}{(Y'-Y)^2} \rightarrow Y \frac{\pi_1 - \pi_2}{\sqrt{\pi_0(1-\pi_0)}} \div \sum X$$

$$\frac{54w}{9} \bowtie \cdots \frac{0}{\sqrt{y}} \sqrt{\frac{\widetilde{}}{RMN_2}} \cdot _o^b = \int \frac{2}{x} \left| \frac{4P^2}{b+C_6} \frac{\sim \sigma^2}{\approx \omega} \cdots \frac{x^{78}}{Y?} \sim \uparrow .95 \right.$$

$$\therefore F = \frac{k}{\sqrt{\partial}} \div \frac{3.1416}{\theta} \cdot \bar{x}\sigma \left(\frac{!!!!}{?} \right) \sqrt{\frac{1234}{5678}} > \frac{H_2O}{CO_2} +$$

$$\left[\frac{H_1}{mOm} \right] \rightarrow \alpha \frac{\nu}{\Delta t + t} \cdot \frac{34}{'44} \div \leftarrow \frac{S^tL\,mo}{\cdots} \left(\frac{!!! \; ee \; \star \, \divideontimes \, \oplus}{-} \right.$$

$$\frac{4}{\sqrt{y^2+r^2}} \cdot \Delta x \cdot P = K(30-v)v = K(30v) - v^2 \frac{\Delta T}{N}\, \theta(2T) +$$

$$-\left(\frac{1}{\pi}\right)^a \infty^2 \rightarrow \frac{\sqrt{\frac{x}{\epsilon a} + \epsilon^{-\frac{x}{a}}}}{du - \frac{1}{2}\nabla} \cdot \int_{\theta_1}^{\theta_2} \sqrt{\frac{d\rho}{d\theta} = \frac{y}{v}} \rightarrow \partial\phi \cdot P \times$$

$$\sqrt{\frac{x-\bar{x}}{\sigma}} \;\|\|\| \; \$\bar{x} \cdot \frac{4}{t}(\not=)\; {}^{3}/_{T} \cdot byx = r_{xy}\frac{\sigma_y}{\sigma_x} \sum_{2}{}^{xy} C''\circ$$

$$\left(\frac{3.49/lb}{\infty}\right)! \sum_{K-3}^{n} \cdot (\oplus) \div \sqrt{\frac{3}{\frac{P.U.}{66}}}\; \nearrow\!\!/\!\!/\; C = Em_2 \Delta \cdot \;\; 3$$

$$18$$

$$3) \;\; x\, a^2 + b^2 = c^2 \;\; \langle 7.65 \rangle \frac{4\cdot 3^2}{1} \cdot \frac{\approx}{\div} \;\; \times\sqrt{9}$$

$$34 \quad \overline{10\cdot 9\cdot 8}$$

$$\female \sqrt{\frac{\leftrightarrow}{\%}} + \hat{\psi} \pm \text{(spiral)} \rightarrow \frac{bc}{Pnt^s} \div \sqrt{\frac{\pi}{3.1416}} \times$$

TERN OF MIND

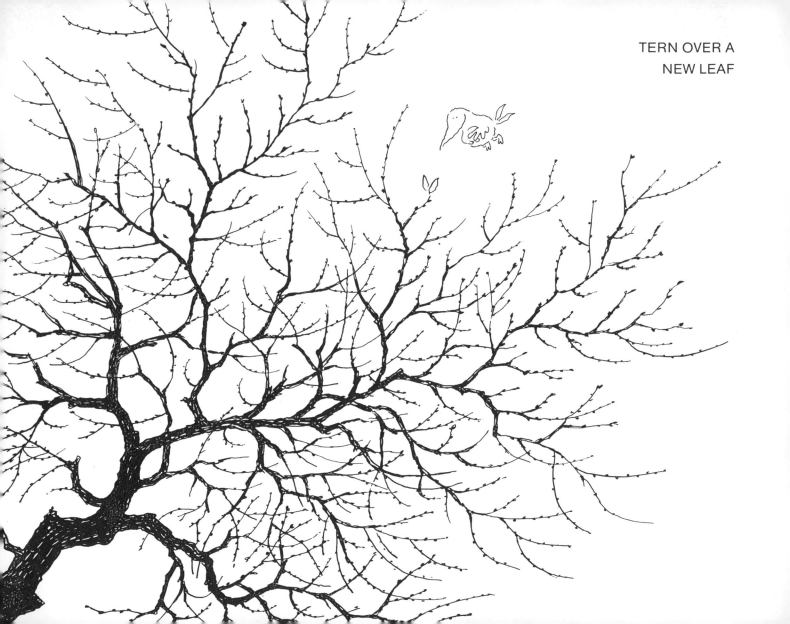

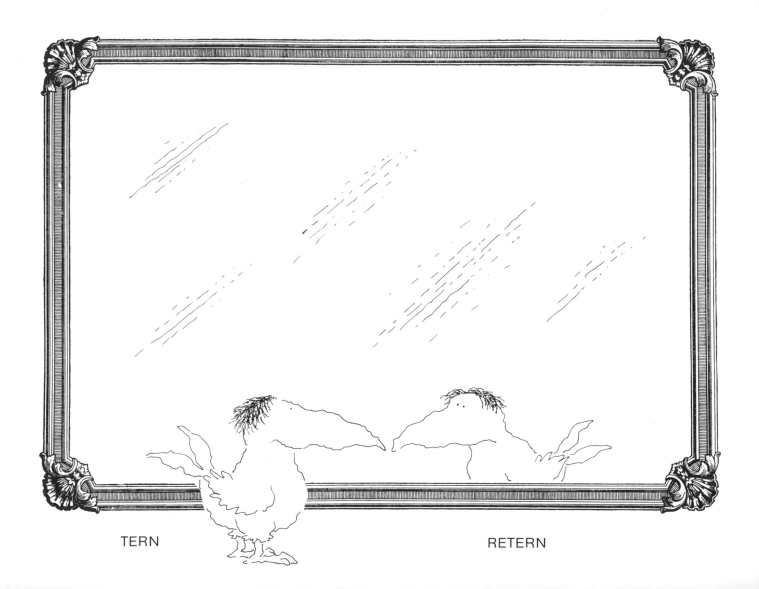

TERN   RETERN

PATTERNS

SATERN

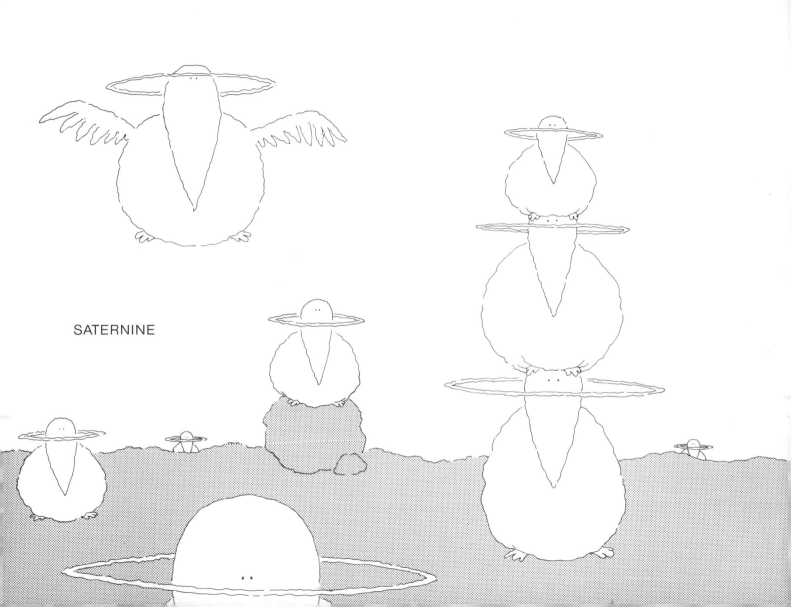

SATERNINE

TERNCOAT

RIGHT TERN

TERN ON A DIME

TOSS AND TERN

TACITERN

TERNABOUT IS FAIR PLAY.

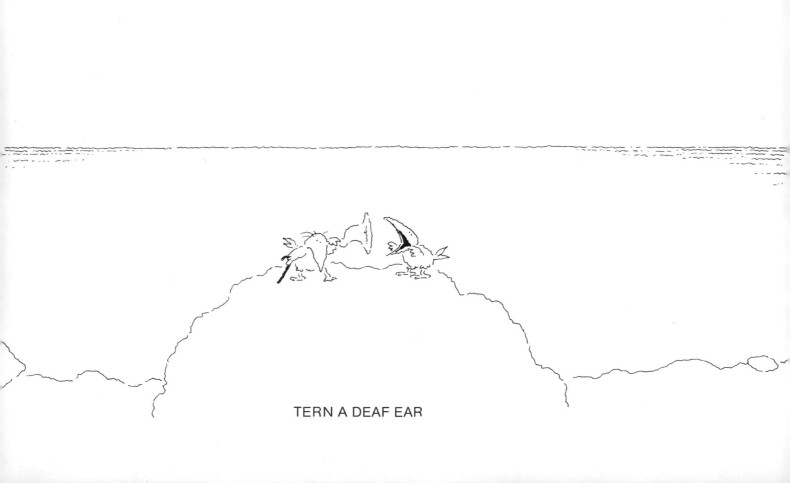

TERN A DEAF EAR

TERN OF EXPRESSION

TERNING SOMERSAULTS

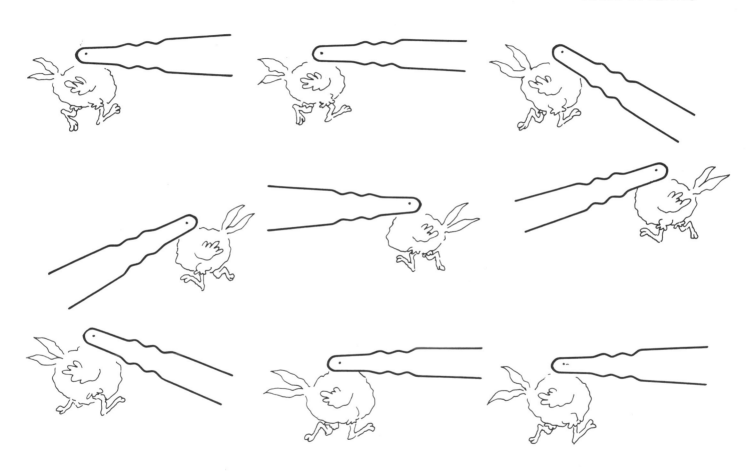

TERN IN THE ROAD

TERN IN THE WEATHER

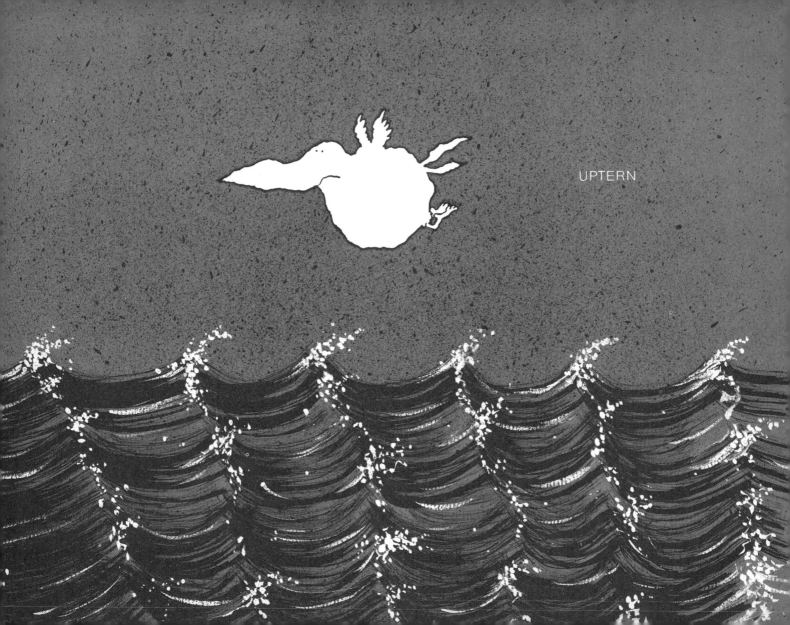

UPTERN

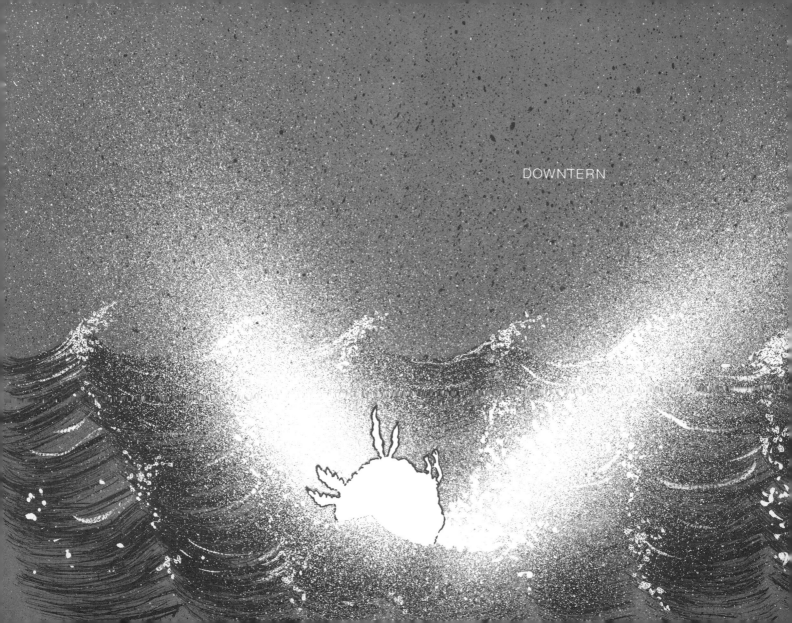

DOWNTERN

SUBALTERNS

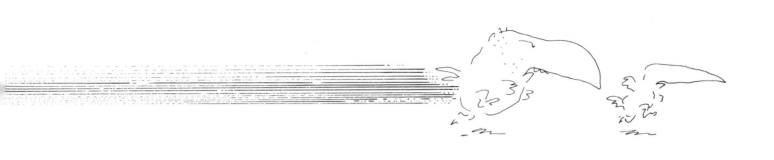

A SUDDEN TERNAROUND

STERN

NO STONE LEFT UNTERNED

TERNING
THE TIDE

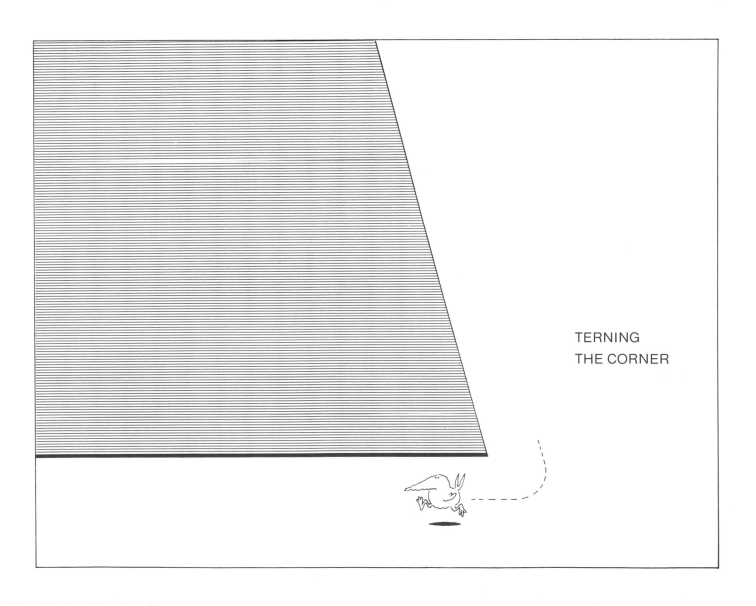

TERNING
THE CORNER

TERN OF
THE CARDS

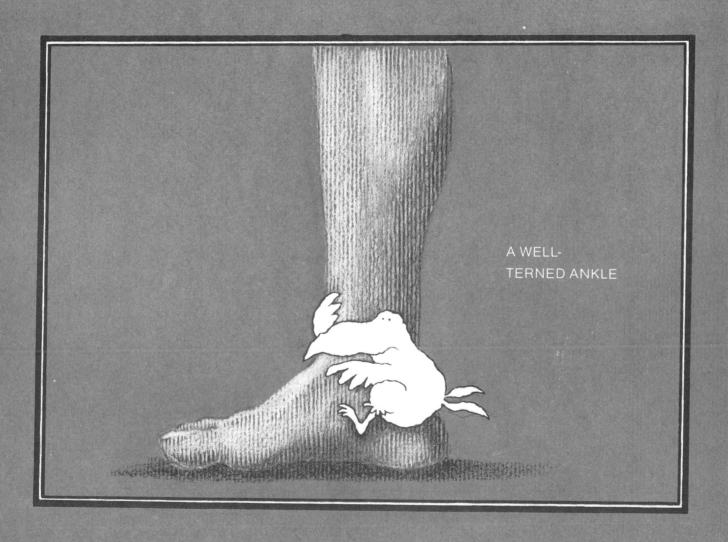

A WELL-
TERNED ANKLE

WAIT
YOUR TERN.

ONE GOOD TERN DESERVES ANOTHER.